SUBHAS
CHANDRA BOSE

LEGENDS AND LEGACIES

THE BIOGRAPHY OF
SUBHAS CHANDRA BOSE

RUPA

Published by
Rupa Publications India Pvt. Ltd 2024
161-B/4, Gulmohar House,
Yusuf Sarai Community Centre,
New Delhi 110049

Sales centres:
Bengaluru Chennai
Hyderabad Kolkata Mumbai

Copyright © Rupa Publications India Pvt. Ltd 2024

The views and opinions expressed in this book are the authors' own and the facts are as reported by him which have been verified to the extent possible, and the publishers are not in any way liable for the same.

All rights reserved.
No part of this publication may be reproduced, transmitted, or stored in a retrieval system, in any form or by any means, electronic, mechanical, photocopying, recording or otherwise, without the prior permission of the publisher.

P-ISBN: 978-93-6156-942-5
E-ISBN: 978-93-6156-258-7

Fourth impression 2026

10 9 8 7 6 5 4

Printed in India

This book is sold subject to the condition that it shall not, by way of trade or otherwise, be lent, resold, hired out, or otherwise circulated, without the publisher's prior consent, in any form of binding or cover other than that in which it is published.

CONTENTS

Introduction 7

1. Importance of Subhas Chandra Bose in Indian History 9
2. 1897–1921: Early life 14
3. Formative Years and Early Political Influences 33
4. Emergence as a Leader in Indian 51
5. 1921–1932: Indian National Congress 63
6. 1937–1940: Indian National Congress 67
7. 1941–1943: Nazi Germany 71
8. 1943–1945: Japanese-occupied Asia 75

INTRODUCTION

Hey there, history buffs and freedom enthusiasts!

Have you ever wondered how a young boy from Cuttack, with an indomitable spirit and an unwavering sense of duty, grew up to challenge the mighty British Empire? Let me introduce you to Subhas Chandra Bose, affectionately known as Netaji, the man whose relentless pursuit of India's freedom left an indelible mark on the nation's history. He didn't have a cape or superpowers, but his courage and determination ignited the flames of revolution and inspired millions to join the fight for independence.

Imagine growing up in the bustling town of Cuttack, nestled by the Mahanadi River, in a household where the air was filled with intellectual debates and the spirit of nationalism. Born on January 23, 1897, Subhas was the ninth child in a family that deeply valued education and hard work.

As a child, Subhas wasn't your typical quiet boy. He was known for his inquisitive nature and fiery temper. Whether it was excelling in his studies or engaging in spirited discussions about India's future, Subhas always stood out. This competitive spirit, coupled with his insatiable thirst for learning, shaped the future leader within him.

His time at school was marked by both academic excellence and incidents of defiance against injustice. Subhas's early education at the Protestant European School and later at Ravenshaw Collegiate School exposed him to a blend of Western philosophies and Indian traditions, broadening his worldview and deepening his resolve to fight for India's freedom.

At thirteen, Subhas's life took a significant turn when he enrolled at the Presidency College in Calcutta. Here, his nationalistic fervour blossomed, fueled by the writings of Swami Vivekananda and the political climate of Bengal. Subhas's passion for his motherland was further ignited by his interactions with influential leaders and his participation in the burgeoning independence movement. His dedication to the cause was unwavering, even leading to his expulsion from college for his confrontational stance against a British professor.

The teachings of Swami Vivekananda, with their call for selfless service and national pride, left a profound impact on him. These influences, combined with the political environment of the time, moulded Subhas into a fervent patriot and a determined leader.

After graduating from Presidency College, Subhas's quest for knowledge took him to England, where he enrolled at the University of Cambridge. Here, he excelled academically but was continually driven by the desire to return to India and contribute to the freedom struggle. Upon his return, Subhas quickly rose through the ranks of the Indian National Congress, becoming a prominent leader known for his fiery speeches and radical ideas.

Subhas Chandra Bose's journey from a curious and rebellious boy to a towering figure in India's independence movement is a testament to the power of determination, intellectual rigour, and unwavering patriotism. His story continues to inspire millions, reminding us that with courage and conviction, we too can challenge the status quo and strive for a better future.

So, dear adventurers of history, take a page from Netaji's book—stay curious, embrace challenges, and never stop fighting for what you believe in. Who knows? The next great revolution might just be waiting for you to lead it!

1

IMPORTANCE OF SUBHAS CHANDRA BOSE IN INDIAN HISTORY

Subhas Chandra Bose, born on 23 January 1897 and presumed dead on 18 August 1945, was an iconic Indian nationalist whose unyielding spirit and patriotism cemented his status as a hero in the annals of Indian history. However, his controversial alliance with Nazi Germany and Imperial Japan during World War II has left a complicated legacy. The honorific "Netaji," meaning "Respected Leader," was first conferred upon him by Indian soldiers in the Indische Legion in Germany around early 1942 and subsequently adopted by Indians worldwide.

1906 Subhas Chandra Bose as child

The Rise of a Radical Leader

A New Voice in the Indian National Congress

In the late 1920s and early 1930s, Subhas Chandra Bose began to carve out a significant niche within the Indian National Congress. Emerging as a beacon of the younger, more radical faction, his powerful oratory skills and unwavering demand for absolute independence from British colonial rule set him apart from his peers. Bose's vision for India's future was bold and uncompromising, earning him both fervent supporters and formidable adversaries within the political arena.

Ascending to the Presidency

Bose's ascent within the Congress was rapid. By 1938, he had achieved the prestigious position of Congress President, a testament to his growing influence and the widespread appeal of his ideas. His tenure was marked by a series of dynamic initiatives aimed at galvanizing the Indian populace and expediting the struggle for independence. Re-elected in 1939, his leadership, however, soon encountered significant obstacles.

Ideological Clashes and Ouster

Despite his initial successes, Bose's tenure was fraught with ideological clashes. His radical approach increasingly put him at odds with Mahatma Gandhi and the conservative high command of the Congress. Gandhi's philosophy of non-violence and gradualism stood in stark contrast to Bose's aggressive stance and urgency for immediate independence. These differences reached a breaking point in 1939, leading to Bose's resignation from the Congress presidency and subsequent marginalisation within the party.

From House Arrest to Daring Escape

Recognising the threat posed by Bose's radicalism, the British authorities swiftly placed him under house arrest. However, confinement could not quell his indomitable spirit. In a daring and meticulously planned escape in 1940, Bose managed to elude British surveillance, embarking on a clandestine journey that would lead him to seek support from the Axis powers in Europe.

Seeking Allies Among the Axis Powers

Bose's escape was a masterstroke of audacity and strategic brilliance. He traversed a perilous route through Afghanistan and the Soviet Union, eventually arriving in Germany. Here, he sought to leverage the global conflict to India's advantage, forging alliances that he hoped would expedite the downfall of British colonial rule in India. His journey into the heart of the Axis powers marked a new, albeit controversial, chapter in his relentless quest for India's freedom.

Bose in Nazi Germany: A Quest for Support

Arriving in Germany in April 1941, Bose found a surprisingly receptive, albeit ambivalent, audience among the Nazi leadership. The Germans, despite their colonial ambitions elsewhere, expressed unexpected sympathy for India's struggle for independence. With German support, Bose established the Free India Centre in Berlin in November 1941, followed by the launch of Free India Radio, which broadcast his impassioned speeches nightly. Concurrently, the formation of the Free India Legion, composed of 3,000 Indian prisoners of war from Erwin Rommel's Afrika Korps, signalled a potential military collaboration for an invasion of India.

A Stamp of Subhas Chandra Bose

Credits: Aaa232355, CC BY-SA 4.0 <https://creativecommons.org/licenses/by-sa/4.0>, via Wikimedia Commons

Shifting Sands: From Germany to Southeast Asia

By 1942, the tide of war and shifting priorities rendered a German invasion of India impractical. Bose, ever adaptive, sought new opportunities in Southeast Asia, aligning more closely with Japan. His single meeting with Adolf Hitler in late May 1942 culminated in an arrangement for Bose to be transported to Asia via a German submarine. During this tumultuous period, Bose's personal life also saw significant developments; his partner, Emilie Schenkl, whom he had met in 1934, gave birth to their daughter in November 1942.

A New Front in Southeast Asia: Reviving the INA

Transferring from a German to a Japanese submarine, Bose arrived in Japanese-occupied Sumatra in May 1943. With Japanese support, he revitalised the Indian National Army (INA), initially composed of Indian POWs from the British Indian Army captured during the Battle of Singapore. Bose's charisma and fervent patriotism attracted thousands of Indian civilians from Malaya and Singapore to join the cause. Under his leadership, the Provisional Government of Free India was established in the Japanese-occupied Andaman and Nicobar Islands.

The INA's Struggle and Decline

Despite his visionary leadership and the INA's remarkable diversity, Bose's military campaign faced insurmountable challenges. The Japanese military, though supportive, considered Bose militarily inexperienced. By late 1944 and early 1945, the British Indian Army had decisively repelled the Japanese offensive, inflicting heavy casualties on both the Japanese and

INA forces. The INA, retreating down the Malay Peninsula, ultimately surrendered with the fall of Singapore. Bose, refusing to capitulate, attempted to flee to Manchuria, hoping to find a new ally in the Soviet Union, which he believed was turning against the British.

The Tragic End and Enduring Mystery

Tragically, Bose's journey ended when he suffered fatal third-degree burns in a plane crash in Taiwan. However, rumours and skepticism surrounding his death persisted, with many Indians, particularly in Bengal, clinging to the hope that he would return to lead India to freedom.

> **Fun Fact:**
> **Early Education:**
> Subhas Chandra Bose was a brilliant student who secured second place in the Calcutta province's matriculation examination. His early education laid a strong foundation for his future revolutionary activities.

A Contested Legacy

Subhas Chandra Bose's life and legacy remain subjects of intense debate and admiration, embodying the complex interplay of patriotism, radicalism, and the quest for independence. His story is a testament to the indomitable spirit of a nation striving for freedom.

2
1897−1921: EARLY LIFE

The Humble Beginnings

In the lively and historic town of Cuttack, nestled by the mighty Mahanadi River, a significant event unfolded on January 23, 1897. At 12:10 PM, Prabhavati Dutt Bose and Janakinath Bose, an advocate from a respected Kayastha family, welcomed their ninth child into the world. This child, born into a well-to-do family of fourteen children, was none other than Subhas Chandra Bose, a name that would later resonate profoundly in the annals of Indian history.

> **Fun Fact:**
> **Presidency College Incident:**
> While at Presidency College, Bose was expelled for assaulting Professor Oaten, who had made a racist remark against Indian students. This incident marked the beginning of Bose's fight against British colonialism.

Cuttack, with its rich heritage and cultural vibrancy, played a pivotal role in shaping the early years of young Subhas. The town, though modest in size, was a hub of political and cultural activities, creating an environment that subtly yet powerfully influenced the impressionable mind of the young boy. The Boses, well-regarded in the community, provided Subhas with a solid foundation in both academics and spirituality, fostering a sense of discipline and a quest for knowledge that set him apart from his peers.

Janakinath Bose, a successful lawyer, and his wife, Prabhavati Devi, a devout and orthodox woman, instilled in their children the values of hard work, integrity, and dedication. These values, combined with the intellectual and cultural richness of Cuttack, nurtured Subhas's growing sense of curiosity and his relentless pursuit of knowledge. Even as a child, Subhas exhibited a keen intellect and an insatiable thirst for learning, qualities that would define his future endeavours.

The town of Cuttack, with its confluence of tradition and modernity, served as a fertile ground for the development of Subhas's early ideals. The cultural tapestry of the town, woven with threads of historical significance and contemporary relevance, influenced his budding sense of nationalism and his emerging vision for an independent India. The vibrant

Amiya Nath Bose, Subhas Chandra Bose and Sisir Kumar Bose at Giddha Pahar, June, 1936

atmosphere of Cuttack, coupled with his family's values, sowed the seeds of patriotism and a deep sense of duty towards his motherland in Subhas's young mind.

As Subhas grew, these seeds took root and flourished, propelling him towards a life dedicated to the pursuit of India's freedom. The confluence of his family's influence, the cultural richness of Cuttack, and his own innate qualities shaped the foundation of a future leader. Subhas Chandra Bose, later known as Netaji, would rise to become one of the most esteemed and revered leaders of India's struggle for independence, leaving an indelible mark on the history of the nation.

Cultural and Political Influences

Cuttack, despite its modest size, was a hub of political and cultural activities that subtly influenced the impressionable Subhas. The atmosphere of the town, combined with the values instilled by his family, sowed the seeds of patriotism and a deep sense of duty towards his motherland. These early influences would grow and flourish, propelling him towards a life dedicated to the pursuit of India's freedom.

> **Fun Fact:**
>
> **ICS Resignation:** Despite securing the fourth rank in the Indian Civil Services (ICS) examination in 1920, Bose resigned from the prestigious post, citing that he could not serve the British government.

The Influence of Education

Subhas Chandra Bose's educational journey began in January 1902 when he was admitted to the Protestant European School in Cuttack, now known as Stewart High School. Like his brothers and sisters, he attended this institution, which was run by the Baptist Mission, until 1909. During these formative years, Subhas was immersed in Western literature, philosophy, and science. This early exposure played a pivotal role in shaping his intellectual and philosophical outlook, broadening his understanding of the world and its myriad complexities. The rigorous curriculum and diverse subject matter instilled in him a disciplined approach to learning and a deep appreciation for knowledge.

Ancestral House of Netaji Subhas Chandra Bose

Credits: Indrajit Das, CC BY-SA 3.0 <https://creativecommons.org/licenses/by-sa/3.0>, via Wikimedia Commons

In 1909, Subhas shifted to Ravenshaw Collegiate School, where he continued to excel academically. His hard work paid off when he secured the second position in the matriculation examination in 1913. Following this achievement, he was admitted to Presidency College, where he studied briefly. Despite his academic success, it was the teachings of Swami Vivekananda and Ramakrishna, whose works he read at the age of sixteen, that profoundly influenced Subhas. He felt that his religion and the philosophy espoused by these great teachers were more important than his studies.

Vivekananda's profound message of selfless service and unwavering dedication to the motherland resonated deeply with Subhas. The sage's call for a life devoted to the upliftment of the downtrodden and the pursuit of national pride struck a profound chord within him, further igniting his fervent spark of nationalism. Vivekananda's teachings offered Subhas a spiritual and philosophical framework that complemented his academic pursuits. The emphasis on serving humanity and fostering a deep love for India provided him with a sense of purpose and direction.

Netaji Subhas Chandra Bose Reviewing the Troops of Azad Hind Fauj-1940's

This powerful mix of Western education and Indian spiritual philosophy provided him with a distinctive perspective, blending rational intellect with a great sense of duty towards his country. He received this unique perspective as a result of this powerful combination. His education was not merely a pursuit of academic excellence but became a journey towards understanding his role in the broader struggle for India's independence. The blend of Western intellectual rigour and Indian spiritual wisdom forged a path that would lead Subhas Chandra Bose to become one of the most iconic leaders in the history of India's fight for freedom.

> **Fun Fact:**
> **Influence of Swami Vivekananda:** Bose was deeply influenced by the teachings of Swami Vivekananda. He believed in the spiritual nationalism propagated by Vivekananda, which guided his revolutionary path.

In those days, the British in Calcutta often made offensive remarks to Indians in public places and insulted them openly. This behaviour of the British, coupled with the outbreak of World War I, began to profoundly influence Subhas Chandra Bose's thinking. The blatant racism and condescension exhibited by the British towards the Indian populace were not merely isolated incidents but a systematic practice aimed at reinforcing their colonial dominance. Such acts of humiliation and disrespect stirred within Subhas a growing sense of indignation and a deep-seated desire to challenge the oppressive regime.

The seeds of nationalism, sown through Vivekananda's inspirational words, began to take root and flourish within Subhas during these tumultuous times. His nationalistic temperament became evident during his time at Presidency College, where he encountered an incident that would mark a significant turning point in his life. Subhas was expelled from the college for allegedly assaulting Professor Oaten, who had manhandled some Indian students for their anti-British comments. Despite his appeal that he merely witnessed the assault and did not participate in it, he was expelled, highlighting the unjust treatment meted out to Indians by the colonial administration.

This incident, while a setback, further solidified Subhas's resolve and commitment to the cause of Indian independence. The unjust expulsion did not deter him; instead, it ignited a fierce determination to continue his education and fight against the colonial injustices. Subhas subsequently joined the Scottish Church College at the University of Calcutta, where he pursued his studies with renewed vigour. He passed his B.A. in philosophy in 1918, a discipline that further deepened his understanding of the complex interplay between Western thought and Indian spiritual philosophies.

> **Fun Fact:**
> **Formation of Forward Bloc:** In 1939, after his resignation from the Indian National Congress due to ideological differences, Bose formed the Forward Bloc to consolidate the anti-British forces in India.

The teachings of Swami Vivekananda and Ramakrishna, which he had embraced at the age of sixteen, continued to be a guiding force in his life. Vivekananda's message of selfless service and dedication to the motherland resonated deeply with Subhas, reinforcing his commitment to the nationalist cause. The sage's call for a life devoted to the upliftment of the downtrodden and the pursuit of national pride struck a profound chord within him, further igniting his fervent spark of nationalism.

Subhas's education was not merely a pursuit of academic excellence but a journey towards understanding his role in the broader struggle for India's independence. The powerful combination of Western education and Indian spiritual philosophy equipped him with a unique perspective, blending rational thought with a profound sense of duty towards his country. This synthesis of intellectual rigour and spiritual wisdom forged a path that would lead Subhas Chandra Bose to become one of the most iconic leaders in the history of

India's fight for freedom.

The experience at Presidency College, coupled with his subsequent academic achievements, shaped Subhas's outlook and fortified his resolve. He realised that true education went beyond the confines of textbooks and classrooms; it was about developing a comprehensive understanding of one's duties and responsibilities towards society. This realization propelled him to actively participate in the nationalist movement, where he employed his education to articulate the aspirations and grievances of the Indian people.

Young Subash Chandra Bose.

Subhas's time at Scottish Church College was marked by a deep engagement with both Western and Indian philosophical traditions. He meticulously studied the works of Western philosophers, juxtaposing them with the teachings of Indian

Bust of Subhas Chandra Bose at Netaji Museum and Centre for Studies in Himalayan Languages Society & Culture

sages like Vivekananda and Ramakrishna. This comparative approach enriched his understanding and provided him with a holistic view of the world, enabling him to formulate strategies that combined intellectual sophistication with spiritual resilience.

His academic journey culminated in a degree in philosophy, but its impact was far-reaching, extending into every aspect of his life and work. Subhas's education became a cornerstone of his leadership, guiding him as he navigated the complex political landscape of colonial India. His ability to blend Western rationality with Indian spirituality became a hallmark of his approach, earning him respect and admiration from a broad spectrum of Indian society.

The seeds of nationalism, nurtured by Vivekananda's teachings and fertilized by his experiences with British injustices, grew into a robust and unyielding commitment to India's independence. Subhas Chandra Bose emerged as a leader whose vision and actions were deeply rooted in his comprehensive education. This unique blend of knowledge and spirituality not only defined his personal journey but also significantly influenced the course of India's struggle for freedom.

The Cambridge Stories

Subhas Chandra Bose embarked on a transformative journey when he left India on September 15, 1919, just weeks before the signing of the Armistice that concluded World War I. Although the war had dragged on, its effects on the everyday lives of Indians were not overtly noticeable. Even the Jallianwala Bagh massacre, which had already taken place, remained shrouded in secrecy, its horrifying details unknown to the general public, including Subhas.

Upon arriving in England, Subhas was singularly focused on his studies. He had promised his father to sit for the Indian

Civil Service (ICS) examination, a commitment that required mastering an intimidating array of subjects: English History, European History, Economics, Geography, Political Science, English Law, Philosophy, Sanskrit, and English Composition. These were subjects not taught in depth in India, leaving Subhas to confront a steep learning curve. Undeterred, he plunged into his studies with relentless dedication, often isolating himself to maintain his rigorous schedule. His colleague at Cambridge, the late C. C. Desai, recalled how difficult it was to coax Subhas out even for a brief walk, so absorbed was he in his academic pursuits.

> **Fun Fact:**
>
> **Azad Hind Radio:** Bose established Azad Hind Radio in Germany to broadcast news and his speeches to Indians in Southeast Asia and India, urging them to join the fight for independence.

For eight months, Subhas worked with intense concentration, his efforts culminating in an impressive fourth-place finish in the ICS examination. This achievement, however, presented a profound dilemma: Should he accept a position under the British Government, or should he dedicate his life to the service of his country? This question gnawed at Subhas, prompting him to seek counsel from the eminent Bengali leader, C. R. Das.

Subhas initiated a profound correspondence with Das, laying bare his personal and spiritual quandaries. In a letter dated February 16, 1921, he expressed his aspirations and sought guidance: "I should like to know what work you may be able to allot to me in this great program of national service. I believe I have the enthusiasm of youth and some education in Philosophy, Economics, Political Science, History, Law, and more. On my return, I aim to engage in teaching and journalism, and to contribute meaningfully to the Congress' activities."

He envisioned establishing a permanent base for the Congress, complete with dedicated research and intelligence departments, comprehensive policies on national issues, and extensive propaganda efforts to educate the masses in various provincial languages. Subhas's letters demonstrated his analytical prowess and unwavering resolve, qualities that would define his future endeavours.

Subhas Chandra Bose 1964 stamp of India

Credits: India Post, Government of India, GODL-India <https://data.gov.in/sites/default/files/Gazette_Notification_OGDL.pdf>, via Wikimedia Commons

Subhas's time at Cambridge was transformative. Though he was deeply immersed in his studies, the intellectual environment and his interactions with peers like Dilip Kumar Roy and C. C. Desai were instrumental in broadening his perspective. These friendships fostered debates that honed his ideological clarity and determination. The contrast between the freedom he witnessed in England and the oppression in India fueled his commitment to India's liberation.

Despite the initial disapproval from his circle of nationalist friends back in Calcutta, who viewed his departure to England as a betrayal, Subhas's experiences at Cambridge proved invaluable. His exposure to diverse ideas and rigorous academic training equipped him with the tools to critically assess and tackle India's challenges. Cambridge, in many ways, molded him into the resolute leader he would become.

Subhas's admiration for certain British qualities, despite his opposition to their imperial rule, is noteworthy. His disciplined approach and sense of honour, which he later instilled in the Indian National Army (INA), mirrored British organizational prowess.

This paradoxical blend of anti-imperial fervour and appreciation for British discipline perplexed many, but it underscored Subhas's nuanced understanding of effective leadership.

The camaraderie and intellectual exchanges at Cambridge left a lasting impact on Subhas. His friendships, debates, and relentless pursuit of knowledge laid the foundation for his future path. The blend of Indian and British influences shaped a unique outlook, making Subhas Chandra Bose a formidable force in India's struggle for independence. His Cambridge chapter was not just an academic sojourn; it was a crucible where his ideals were forged and his resolve steeled for the battles ahead.

> **Fun Fact:**
> **Azad Hind Fauj (Indian National Army):** Bose reorganised the Indian National Army (INA) with the help of Japan during World War II. The INA aimed to liberate India from British rule through armed struggle.

The context of Subhas's departure from India is significant. The country was in a state of turmoil, with the British Raj tightening its grip and the freedom movement gaining momentum. The Jallianwala Bagh massacre had left a scar on the national psyche, but the full extent of its brutality was not yet known. Gandhi, deeply moved by the incident, was beginning to mobilize the masses, travelling across the country to gauge the reaction of the people. In this charged atmosphere, Subhas's departure to England seemed a retreat, but it was, in fact, a strategic move to arm himself with

Subhas Chandra Bose 1964 stamp of India

Credits: India Post, Government of India, GODL-India <https:// data.gov.in/sites/default/files/ Gazette_Notification_OGDL.pdf>, via Wikimedia Commons

the knowledge and credentials needed to fight for India's freedom more effectively.

At Cambridge, Subhas's life was a study in contrasts. On one hand, he was engrossed in his studies, rarely stepping out of his rigorous academic routine. On the other hand, he was in constant intellectual engagement with his peers. His letters to C. R. Das reveal a mind in turmoil, grappling with the weighty decision of whether to join the ICS or to devote his life to national service. This period of intense self-reflection and ideological crystallization was crucial in shaping his future path.

Subhas's correspondence with Das is a window into his soul, reflecting his earnestness and depth of conviction. In his letter dated March 2, 1921, he outlined a detailed plan for his future involvement in the national movement:

These letters are illustrative of a phase in Subhas's life that sheds light on many of the daring and original actions he undertook later. They reveal a young man who had transcended his adolescence, leaving behind the uncertainties of youth for a resolute manhood. The letters highlight his determination to find solutions to the problems he faced and his commitment to following through on his decisions without equivocation.

> **Fun Fact:**
> **Provisional Government of Free India:** On October 21, 1943, Bose announced the formation of the Provisional Government of Free India in Singapore, which was recognised by several Axis powers.

Subhas's time at Cambridge was marked by intense debate and discussion with contemporaries, teachers, and acquaintances. These interactions played a significant role in shaping his worldview and preparing him for his future role in India's struggle for independence. While in India, his thoughts and debates often remained speculative and within the realm of fantasy, his letters from Cambridge reflect a shift towards concrete and purposeful conclusions.

The influence of Cambridge on Subhas's personality cannot be underestimated. Although his stay there was relatively short and focused primarily on preparing for exams, the time spent and the friendships made were crucial in shaping his moral and intellectual outlook. Subhas's loyalty to his nationalist circle in Calcutta, despite their disapproval of his departure to England, speaks to his deep sense of commitment and the personal sacrifices he was willing to make for the greater good.

The friendships he formed at Cambridge, particularly with Dilip Kumar Roy and C. C. Desai, were instrumental in his development. These relationships provided a platform for rigorous intellectual engagement, fostering an environment where ideas could be freely exchanged and debated. This intellectual camaraderie enriched Subhas's mind and helped solidify his ideological stance.

Subhas's exposure to British culture and education at Cambridge also played a significant role in shaping his leadership style. While he remained firmly opposed to British imperialism, he admired certain British qualities, such as their organizational skills and sense of discipline. These attributes influenced his later efforts to instill a similar sense of order and discipline in the Indian National Army (INA). This nuanced appreciation of British qualities, despite his political opposition, highlights Subhas's ability to critically assess and adopt positive aspects from different cultures.

> **Fun Fact:**
> **Singapore Rally:** At a massive rally in Singapore in July 1943, Bose gave the famous slogan "Give me blood, and I shall give you freedom," which inspired thousands to join the INA.

Subhas's stay at Cambridge also opened his eyes to the broader world. The contrast between the freedom he witnessed in England and the oppression in India made a profound impact on him. He realized that for India to achieve parity with other nations, it needed to embrace progress and reform its social systems. This realization fueled his determination to fight for India's liberation and modernize its social and political structures.

Subhas Chandra Bose addressing a meeting in Berlin in 1933

The writer C. C. Desai often spoke of the deep bond he shared with Subhas and the profound impact Subhas had on his life. Desai's admiration for Subhas was evident, and he often remarked on the shame he felt for not being able to match Subhas's level of dedication to the national cause. This sentiment was shared by many of Subhas's contemporaries, who recognized his extraordinary commitment and the sacrifices he made for India's freedom.

Subhas's stay at Cambridge was not without its challenges. The pressure of academic rigour, coupled with the ideological struggle he faced, tested his resolve. However, these challenges also strengthened his character and prepared him for the formidable task of leading India's fight for independence. The intellectual and personal growth he experienced at Cambridge laid the foundation for his future actions and decisions.

Subhas's nuanced understanding of British culture and his ability to adopt and adapt positive aspects from it, while firmly opposing British imperialism, is a testament to his pragmatic and strategic approach to leadership. This ability to balance ideological purity with practical considerations made him a formidable leader in India's struggle for independence.

> **Fun Fact:**
>
> **Bose and Hitler:** During World War II, Bose sought assistance from Nazi Germany to fight British colonial rule. He met Adolf Hitler in 1942, although their meeting did not yield significant support.

Challenges and Growing Nationalism

During his time at Presidency College, Subhas encountered firsthand the racial prejudices and injustices perpetrated by the British. The offensive remarks and open insults directed at Indians in public places by the British in Calcutta were commonplace. Such behaviour, coupled with the outbreak of World War I, profoundly influenced Subhas's thinking and solidified his growing sense of nationalism.

His nationalistic temperament became evident when he was expelled from Presidency College for allegedly assaulting Professor Oaten, who had manhandled some Indian students for their anti-British comments. Despite his appeal that he merely witnessed the assault and did not participate in it, he was expelled, highlighting the unjust treatment meted out to Indians by the colonial administration.

This incident, while a setback, further solidified Subhas's resolve and commitment to the cause of Indian independence.

The unjust expulsion did not deter him; instead, it ignited a fierce determination to continue his education and fight against the colonial injustices. Subhas subsequently joined the Scottish Church College at the University of Calcutta, where he pursued his studies with renewed vigour. He passed his B.A. in philosophy in 1918, a discipline that further deepened his understanding of the complex interplay between Western thought and Indian spiritual philosophies.

Journey to Europe and Further Education

In his quest for higher education and to fulfil a promise made to his father, Subhas left India for Europe on September 15, 1919, arriving in London on October 20. His father had provided Rs 10,000 for him to prepare and appear for the Indian Civil Services (ICS) examination. In London, Subhas stayed in Belsize Park with his brother Satish, who was preparing for the bar exam. This period was crucial in expanding Subhas's horizons and exposing him to new ideas and experiences.

Tribute to Subhas Chandra Bose on 23 January 2021 in South Kolkata, India

Credits: Titodutta, CC0, via Wikimedia Commons

According to historian Leonard A. Gordon, Subhas's Civil Service application demonstrates his family's connectedness to the small, interrelated elite of Bengal. For references, he provided the names of the two highest-ranking Indians in the councils of the British-Indian establishment: Lord Sinha of Raipur, Under Secretary of State for India and the first Indian to serve as governor of a province under the Raj, and Mr. Bhupendranath Basu, a wealthy Calcutta solicitor and a member of the Council of India in London.

Subhas was eager to gain admission to a college at the University of Cambridge. However, it was already past the deadline for admission. With the help of some Indian students there and Mr. Reddaway, the Censor of Fitzwilliam Hall—a body run by the Non-Collegiate Students Board of the university, which made the university's education available at an economical cost without formal admission to a college—Subhas entered the register of the university on November 19, 1919. He chose the Mental and Moral Sciences Tripos and simultaneously set about preparing for the Civil Service exams.

> **Fun Fact:**
> **Role in WWII:** Bose's INA fought alongside Japanese forces against the British in the Burma Campaign. Despite initial successes, the campaign ended in failure due to supply issues and the onset of the monsoon.

The early years of Subhas Chandra Bose were marked by a unique blend of academic rigour, spiritual growth, and an unyielding quest for knowledge. These formative experiences, coupled with the cultural and political influences of his environment, laid the groundwork for his future role as a revolutionary leader in India's struggle for independence. The seeds of patriotism sown in his early years would grow and flourish, driving him towards a life of sacrifice and relentless pursuit of freedom for his motherland.

The Decision to Fight for Independence

Subhas came fourth in the ICS examination and was selected, but he did not want to work under an alien government, which would mean serving the British. As he stood on the verge of taking the plunge by resigning from the Indian Civil Service in 1921, he wrote to his elder brother Sarat Chandra Bose: "Only on the soil of sacrifice and suffering can we raise our national edifice."

True to his words, Subhas resigned from his civil service job on April 23, 1921, and returned to India. His resignation marked a significant turning point in his life, symbolising his unwavering commitment to the cause of Indian independence. This decision was not taken lightly, as it involved a great personal sacrifice. However, Subhas was driven by a deep-seated belief that true freedom could only be achieved through selfless sacrifice and relentless struggle.

> **Fun Fact:**
> **Death Controversy:** Bose's death in a plane crash in 1945 remains a subject of controversy and speculation. Various theories suggest he may have survived and lived in disguise.

A Unique Blend of Knowledge and Spirituality

Throughout his journey, Subhas's education remained a cornerstone of his leadership. His ability to blend Western rationality with Indian spirituality became a hallmark of his approach, earning him respect and admiration from a broad spectrum of Indian society. The seeds of nationalism, nurtured by Vivekananda's teachings and fertilised by his experiences with British injustices, grew into a robust and unyielding commitment to India's independence.

Bose whose vision and actions were deeply rooted in his comprehensive education. This unique blend of knowledge and spirituality not only defined his personal journey but also significantly influenced the course of.

3

FORMATIVE YEARS AND EARLY POLITICAL INFLUENCES

Early Influences and Inspirations

Subhas Chandra Bose's early life and formative years were profoundly influenced by a confluence of cultural, intellectual, and familial factors that collectively shaped his political trajectory. Subhas belonged to a well-respected Bengali family. His father, Janaki Nath Bose, was a prominent lawyer and a staunch advocate for Indian rights under British rule. Janaki Nath's prominence in society exposed young Subhas to a milieu replete with intellectual vigour and political discourse, which were instrumental in shaping his burgeoning nationalistic sentiments.

> **Fun Fact:**
> **Legacy in Japan:** Bose is revered in Japan for his efforts against British colonialism. Several memorials and monuments in his honour can be found in Japan, reflecting the deep respect he garnered.

The Bose family was a blend of traditional Indian values and modern intellectual pursuits. Janaki Nath Bose's influence extended beyond his professional achievements; he was also a notable figure in various social reform movements. This environment at home was rich in discussions about national issues, the importance of education, and the need for social reforms. Subhas's mother, Prabhavati Devi, a deeply religious woman, inculcated in him a sense of spiritual duty and moral rectitude. Her devotion to traditional Indian values balanced the Western ideas that Subhas encountered in his formal education.

Subhas's early education began at the Protestant European School in Cuttack, where he was exposed to Western philosophies and ideas. However, it was his subsequent enrollment at Ravenshaw Collegiate School that had a more profound impact. Here, he came under the tutelage of Beni Madhav Das, the headmaster, whose profound influence on Subhas was unparalleled. Das was a remarkable educator who not only imparted academic knowledge but also inspired his students with ideas of nationalism and pride in their heritage. His teachings ignited in Subhas a passion for Indian culture and history, instilling in him a sense of duty towards the nation.

> **Fun Fact:**
> **INA Trials:** The trials of INA officers by the British in 1945-46 galvanised Indian public opinion and played a crucial role in strengthening the demand for independence.

The socio-political environment of Bengal during Subhas's formative years was a crucible of revolutionary ideas and cultural renaissance. The writings of Bankim Chandra Chattopadhyay, with his evocative novel "Anandamath" and the hymn "Vande Mataram," stirred a sense of nationalism among the youth. Swami Vivekananda's teachings were particularly influential for Subhas. Vivekananda's emphasis on spiritual nationalism, the idea of service to the motherland as a divine duty, and the call for the youth to rise and build a strong and self-reliant India resonated deeply with Subhas. He was inspired by Vivekananda's vision of an India that combined spiritual wisdom with modern scientific advancements.

Rabindranath Tagore's contributions to the Bengali cultural renaissance also left a lasting impression on Subhas. Tagore's literary works, imbued with themes of freedom and human dignity, and his efforts in educational reforms through institutions like Visva-Bharati University at Santiniketan, provided a model of intellectual independence and cultural pride. Subhas admired Tagore's holistic approach to education, which emphasised the development of a free-thinking and culturally rooted individual.

Subhas's intellectual growth was not confined to the classroom. The political climate of the time, marked by the rise of the Indian National Congress and the Swadeshi Movement, played a crucial role in shaping his political consciousness. The partition of Bengal in 1905 by Lord Curzon had sparked

Ancestral House of Netaji Subhas Chandra Bose

Credits: Indrajit Das, CC BY-SA 3.0 <https://creativecommons.org/licenses/by-sa/3.0>, via Wikimedia Commons

widespread protests and a revival of nationalistic fervor. Subhas, though young, was deeply moved by the events around him. The boycott of British goods, the promotion of indigenous industries, and the collective spirit of resistance against colonial policies left an indelible mark on his young mind.

> **Fun Fact:**
> **Influence on Indian Armed Forces:** The INA's struggle and sacrifices inspired many within the Indian Armed Forces, contributing to the growing discontent and eventual end of British rule.

As Subhas transitioned from adolescence to adulthood, his exposure to various revolutionary ideas expanded. His elder brother, Sarat Chandra Bose, who was also deeply involved in the freedom struggle, became a mentor and a source of inspiration. Sarat's involvement with the Anushilan Samiti, a secret revolutionary society in Bengal, introduced Subhas to more radical approaches to achieving independence. The discussions and debates at home about the efficacy of different strategies for India's liberation helped Subhas develop a nuanced understanding of the complexities involved in the struggle against British rule.

Subhas's academic journey took a significant turn when he went to Calcutta to attend the Presidency College. His experience at Presidency was a mix of academic rigour and political awakening. The college was a hub of intellectual activity and nationalist fervour. It was here that Subhas first encountered organised student movements and the spirit of defiance against colonial authority. His expulsion from Presidency College in 1916, for his alleged involvement in an assault on Professor Oaten, who had made derogatory remarks about Indians, was a defining moment. This incident not only highlighted his growing commitment to the national cause but also his willingness to confront injustice directly.

After his expulsion, Subhas continued his studies at the Scottish Church College, where he graduated in 1919 with a degree in philosophy. The philosophical training he received here, particularly in Western philosophical thought, helped him develop a critical and analytical approach to the socio-political issues facing India. His engagement with Western philosophers like Kant, Hegel, and Bergson, and Eastern spiritual texts like the Upanishads and the Bhagavad Gita, provided him with a broad intellectual framework to articulate his vision for India's future.

Subhas's journey to England in 1919, to prepare for the Indian Civil Service (ICS) examination, marked another pivotal phase in his life. The decision to join the ICS was influenced by his father's belief that Indians needed to be part of the administrative machinery to bring about change from within. Subhas excelled in the examination, securing the fourth rank. However, his time in England exposed him to the dichotomy between the British democratic ideals and the reality of colonial rule in India. The racism and condescension he encountered in England further fueled his resolve to fight for India's independence.

While in England, Subhas's engagement with the Indian student community and various political groups deepened his

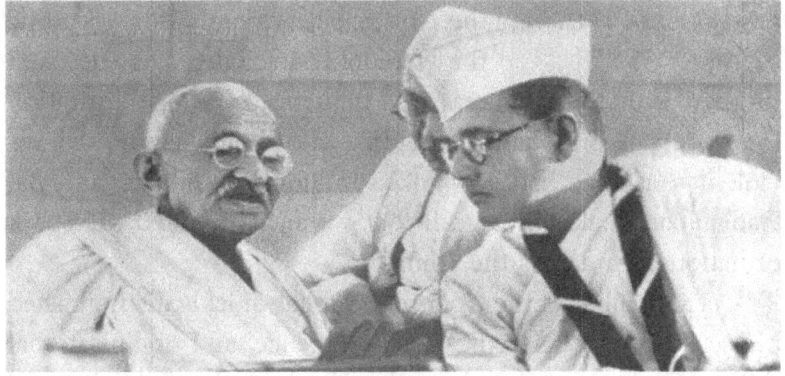

Gandhi at the Indian National Congress annual meeting in Haripura in 1938 with Congress President Subhas Chandra Bose.

understanding of international politics and the global anti-colonial movement. He was influenced by the writings and speeches of Irish nationalist leaders like Eamon de Valera and the Sinn Féin movement, which sought complete independence from British rule. The parallels between the Irish struggle and the Indian freedom movement reinforced his belief in the necessity of radical approaches to achieve independence.

Subhas's return to India in 1921 marked the beginning of his full-time involvement in the national movement. His resignation from the ICS, a coveted and prestigious position, was a bold and symbolic act of defiance against British authority. This decision was not taken lightly; it involved deep introspection and a firm commitment to the cause of India's liberation. Subhas's letters to his family during this period reflect his inner turmoil and his ultimate resolve to dedicate his life to the service of the nation.

Subhas Chandra Bose
Credits: Yokozunakotozakura, CC BY-SA 4.0 <https://creativecommons.org/licenses/by-sa/4.0>, via Wikimedia Commons

Upon his return, Subhas joined the Indian National Congress (INC), the principal organisation leading the freedom struggle. His decision to align with the Congress was influenced by his admiration for leaders like Mahatma Gandhi, whose philosophy of non-violent resistance had galvanized millions of Indians, and Bal Gangadhar Tilak, whose call for Swaraj had ignited the spark of nationalism across the country.

As a member of the Congress, Subhas quickly distinguished himself through his dedication, eloquence, and organisational skills. He was appointed as the Head of the Publicity and

Propaganda Department of the Bengal Provincial Congress Committee. In this role, he utilized his communication skills to garner support for the Congress's activities, mobilising students, workers, and the general public. His ability to articulate the aspirations and grievances of the people made him a powerful voice in the national movement.

Subhas's early political activities were characterised by a blend of idealism and pragmatism. He believed in the importance of building a strong and disciplined organisation capable of challenging British authority. His efforts to mobilise the youth and create a network of volunteers were aimed at creating a robust infrastructure for the freedom struggle. He emphasised the need for self-reliance, urging people to boycott British goods and support indigenous industries.

Throughout this period, Subhas remained deeply influenced by the teachings of Swami Vivekananda and the cultural renaissance in Bengal. His vision of a free India was not just political but also spiritual and cultural. He envisioned an India that combined the wisdom of its ancient traditions with the advancements of modern science and technology. This holistic vision of nation-building would continue to guide his actions and strategies throughout his political career.

> **Fun Fact:**
> **Subhas Chandra Bose Airport:** The international airport in Kolkata is named in his honour, reflecting his enduring legacy and significance in Indian history.

In conclusion, Subhas Chandra Bose's initial political activities were shaped by a rich tapestry of influences, ranging from his family background and early education to the socio-political environment of Bengal and his exposure to Western and Eastern philosophical thought. His early experiences and interactions with prominent leaders and thinkers provided him with the intellectual and ideological foundation for his later contributions to the Indian freedom movement. His journey from a young student imbibing nationalist ideals to a dedicated leader of the Congress marked the beginning of a remarkable political career that would leave an indelible mark on India's struggle for independence.

Role in the Non-Cooperation Movement

Interaction with Mahatma Gandhi

Subhas Chandra Bose's interactions with Mahatma Gandhi were pivotal in shaping his early political career and his approach to the Indian independence movement. These interactions were marked by a complex blend of admiration, ideological divergence, and mutual respect. The dynamics of their relationship played a significant role in the evolution of Bose's political strategies and his eventual divergence from mainstream Congress ideology.

Subhas first met Gandhi in 1921, shortly after his return to India from England. This meeting was a turning point for Bose, who sought Gandhi's guidance on how best to contribute to the freedom struggle. Gandhi, by then, had emerged as the undisputed leader of the Indian National Congress, advocating a philosophy of non-violent resistance (Satyagraha) that had already mobilised millions of Indians. Bose admired Gandhi's ability to inspire and lead, but he also had reservations about the efficacy of strict non-violence as the sole strategy for achieving independence.

During their initial interaction, Bose posed several probing questions to Gandhi about the Congress's strategies and the broader objectives of the non-cooperation movement. He was particularly interested in understanding how non-violence could effectively challenge the deeply entrenched British colonial system. Gandhi's responses, which emphasised moral and spiritual resistance over physical confrontation, did not fully satisfy Bose. Nevertheless, the meeting left a profound impression on him and marked the beginning of his active involvement in the Congress's activities.

Bose's admiration for Gandhi was evident in his early speeches and writings. He frequently praised Gandhi's leadership and the mass mobilisation achieved under his guidance. However, Bose's political philosophy was evolving in a different direction. Influenced by revolutionary movements worldwide, including the Irish struggle for independence and the Bolshevik Revolution in Russia, Bose began to advocate for a more assertive approach to achieving freedom.

The non-cooperation movement of 1920-1922 was a significant phase in Bose's political journey. Gandhi's call for non-violent non-cooperation was a radical departure from previous forms of protest. It involved boycotting British goods, institutions, and honours and refusing to pay taxes. The movement aimed to paralyse the colonial administration through mass civil disobedience, forcing the British to concede to Indian demands.

> **Fun Fact:**
>
> **Philosophy of Militarism:** Bose believed in the necessity of armed struggle to achieve independence. He was critical of Gandhi's non-violent approach, advocating for more aggressive methods.

Bose embraced the movement with fervour, recognising its potential to unite Indians across different social and economic backgrounds. He actively participated in organising protests, boycotts, and public meetings, urging people to reject British authority and embrace self-reliance. His eloquence and passion made him a compelling orator, capable of inspiring large crowds.

However, Bose's revolutionary zeal often put him at odds with Gandhi's strictly non-violent approach. While Gandhi emphasised patience and moral fortitude, Bose believed that more direct and militant actions were necessary to expedite independence. This ideological tension between them became increasingly apparent as the movement progressed.

One of the most significant points of divergence between Bose and Gandhi was their approach to dealing with colonial repression. Gandhi maintained that non-violence was not merely a tactic but a moral imperative. He believed that suffering endured in the pursuit of justice would ultimately awaken the conscience of the oppressor and lead to liberation. Bose, on the other hand, was more pragmatic. He argued that the British, entrenched in their imperialistic ambitions, would not relinquish control without a formidable challenge that included the threat of armed resistance.

Despite these differences, Bose continued to work within the framework of the non-cooperation movement, recognising the strategic advantage of Gandhi's mass appeal. He respected Gandhi's ability to mobilise the rural masses, who formed the backbone of the movement. Bose saw the value in Gandhi's emphasis on swadeshi (self-reliance) and the boycott of British goods, which he believed were essential steps toward economic independence and self-sufficiency.

Signature of Subhas Chandra Bose, Indian freedom fighter and politician.

The Prince of Wales' visit to India in December 1921 provided Bose with an opportunity to translate his revolutionary ideas into action. The Congress, under Gandhi's leadership, decided to boycott the visit as a demonstration of Indian

FORMATIVE YEARS AND EARLY POLITICAL INFLUENCES

discontent with British rule. Bose played a crucial role in organising the boycott in Bengal, particularly in Calcutta, where he mobilised students, workers, and the general public to participate in a massive hartal (strike).

The success of the boycott in Calcutta was a testament to Bose's organisational skills and his ability to galvanise public sentiment. The hartal effectively paralysed the city, showcasing the growing unrest among Indians and their willingness to defy colonial authority. This event marked Bose as a prominent leader in the national movement and brought him into the spotlight of British authorities.

> **Fun Fact:**
> **Escape from British Surveillance:** In 1941, Bose escaped from house arrest in Calcutta, travelling through Afghanistan and the Soviet Union to reach Germany, demonstrating his resourcefulness and determination.

The British response to the boycott was swift and severe. Bose, along with other leaders like Chittaranjan Das, was arrested and imprisoned. This marked Bose's first imprisonment, an experience that profoundly impacted him both personally and politically.

> **Fun Fact:**
> **Haripura Session:** Bose was elected President of the Indian National Congress in 1938 at the Haripura Session, where he emphasised the importance of self-reliance and industrialisation for India's progress.

Boycott of the Prince of Wales' Visit

The boycott of the Prince of Wales' visit to India in December 1921 was a significant event in the Indian independence movement, showcasing the growing defiance against British rule and highlighting the organisational prowess of leaders like Subhas Chandra Bose. This event not only marked a critical juncture in Bose's political career but also underscored the increasing militancy of the Indian National Congress under Gandhi's leadership.

The Prince of Wales, later known as King Edward VIII, embarked on a tour of India as part of a broader effort to bolster support for the British Empire in the aftermath of World War I. The visit was intended to reaffirm the bonds between Britain and its colonies, but it came at a time of heightened political unrest in India. The Non-Cooperation Movement, launched by Gandhi in 1920, had galvanised millions of Indians to reject British authority and embrace self-reliance.

The decision to boycott the Prince's visit was part of the Congress's strategy to demonstrate Indian discontent with

This is the ancestral house of Subhas Chandra Bose is at Shubashgram (Kodalia) near Kolkata.

Credits: Indrajit Das, CC BY-SA 3.0 <https://creativecommons.org/licenses/by-sa/3.0>, via Wikimedia Commons

British rule. Gandhi's call for a hartal (general strike) on the day of the Prince's arrival was a bold move designed to show the extent of Indian resistance. Subhas Chandra Bose, who had recently returned to India and joined the Congress, saw this as an opportunity to assert his leadership and further the cause of independence.

Bose's role in organising the boycott in Bengal, particularly in Calcutta, was instrumental. As the Head of the Publicity and Propaganda Department of the Bengal Provincial Congress Committee, he utilised his communication skills to mobilise support for the hartal. He worked tirelessly to coordinate efforts among students, workers, and various community leaders, ensuring a unified response to the Prince's visit.

> **Fun Fact:**
> **Book "The Indian Struggle":** Bose authored "The Indian Struggle," covering the period from 1920 to 1942. The book provides valuable insights into his thoughts and the Indian freedom movement.

On the day of the Prince's arrival, Calcutta witnessed one of the most significant hartals in its history. Shops and businesses were closed, public transportation came to a halt, and the streets were filled with protestors. Bose's ability to orchestrate such a large-scale demonstration was a testament to his organisational acumen and his ability to inspire and lead. The hartal not only paralysed the city but also sent a powerful message to the British authorities about the growing resolve of the Indian people.

The success of the boycott in Calcutta was a critical moment for Bose. It established him as a key leader within Congress and demonstrated his capability to mobilise mass support. However, it also drew the ire of the British authorities. The colonial government, alarmed by the scale and intensity of the protests, responded with a crackdown on the leaders of the movement.

Bose, along with Chittaranjan Das and other prominent leaders, was arrested and imprisoned. This marked Bose's first imprisonment, an experience that profoundly impacted him both personally and politically. In prison, Bose had the opportunity to reflect on his political beliefs and strategies. He read extensively, deepening his understanding of various political ideologies and revolutionary movements worldwide. This period of incarceration strengthened his resolve and solidified his commitment to India's independence.

The boycott of the Prince of Wales' visit and the subsequent imprisonment of its leaders garnered significant public sympathy and support. Bose and his fellow prisoners were hailed as heroes, and their sacrifices became a rallying point for the national movement. The event also highlighted the growing tension within the Congress regarding the methods of resistance. While Gandhi continued to advocate for strict non-violence, Bose's willingness to confront the authorities directly foreshadowed his future divergence from Gandhi's philosophy.

Janakinath Bose, Bivabati Devi, Subhas Chandra Bose and Sarat Chandra Bose in Shillong, 1927

First Imprisonment and Its Impact

Subhas Chandra Bose's first imprisonment in December 1921 marked a critical turning point in his political career and had a profound impact on his subsequent actions and strategies. This period of incarceration was not merely a personal ordeal but a transformative experience that shaped his ideological stance and reinforced his commitment to the Indian independence movement.

Following his arrest for organizing the boycott of the Prince of Wales' visit, Bose was detained in Alipore Jail in Calcutta. This experience of imprisonment exposed him to the harsh realities of colonial repression and the sacrifices required in the struggle for freedom. Despite the physical and psychological hardships, Bose used his time in prison constructively, turning it into a period of intense intellectual engagement and reflection.

In Alipore Jail, Bose found himself among a diverse group of political prisoners, including seasoned leaders and young

Subhas Chandra Bose visits Andaman Cellular Jail.
Credits: Jansatta newspaper (ed. January 23, 2021), Public domain, via Wikimedia Commons

revolutionaries. This environment provided a fertile ground for discussions and debates on various political ideologies and strategies. Bose engaged in extensive dialogues with his fellow inmates, sharing his views and learning from their experiences. These interactions helped him broaden his understanding of the complexities of the independence movement and the different approaches being advocated by various factions.

Statue of Netaji Subhas Chandra Bose at India Gate Canopy in New Delhi
Credits: Pinakpani, CC BY-SA 4.0 <https://creativecommons.org/licenses/by-sa/4.0>, via Wikimedia Commons

One of the significant influences during this period was his interaction with Chittaranjan Das, a prominent leader of the Congress and Bose's political mentor. Das's unwavering commitment to the cause and his strategic vision left a lasting impression on Bose. Das emphasised the importance of combining non-cooperation with constructive programs like promoting indigenous industries and education. This approach resonated with Bose's belief in the need for a comprehensive strategy to achieve independence.

Bose's time in prison also allowed him to delve deeply into revolutionary literature and the works of political philosophers.

He read extensively about the Russian Revolution, the Irish struggle for independence, and other anti-colonial movements. The writings of Lenin, Trotsky, and other Marxist thinkers provided him with insights into the strategies of revolutionary movements and the role of armed struggle in achieving political objectives. These readings reinforced his belief that non-violence alone might not be sufficient to overthrow the British colonial regime.

The harsh conditions of imprisonment, including poor sanitation, inadequate nutrition, and the constant threat of disease, took a toll on Bose's health. He contracted tuberculosis during his incarceration, which would later necessitate periods of convalescence and treatment. However, these hardships only served to strengthen his resolve and deepen his conviction in the justness of the cause he was fighting for.

> **Fun Fact:**
> **Role in INA Women's Regiment:** Bose formed the Rani of Jhansi Regiment, an all-women combat unit within the INA, symbolising his belief in women's active participation in the freedom struggle.

Bose's release from prison in 1922, after serving a six-month sentence, was met with widespread public acclaim. He was welcomed as a hero, and his stature within the Congress rose significantly. His imprisonment had transformed him from a relatively unknown figure into a prominent leader in the national movement. The experience also steeled him for the many future imprisonments and hardships he would face in his relentless pursuit of India's freedom.

Upon his release, Bose resumed his political activities with renewed vigour. He continued to work closely with Chittaranjan Das and other leaders to advance the cause of non-cooperation.

However, his experiences in prison had also made him more critical of the Congress's strategies. He began to advocate for a more assertive and confrontational approach to British rule, which often put him at odds with the moderate leadership of the Congress.

Bose's imprisonment had a profound impact on his personal philosophy and political strategies. It reinforced his belief in the necessity of a multi-faceted approach to the freedom struggle, combining non-cooperation with the development of indigenous industries, .

This is the ancestral house of Subhas Chandra Bose is at Shubashgram (Kodalia) near Kolkata.

Credits: Indrajit Das, CC BY-SA 3.0 <https://creativecommons.org/licenses/by-sa/3.0>, via Wikimedia Commons

4

EMERGENCE AS A LEADER IN INDIAN INDEPENDENCE MOVEMENT

Leadership in Bengal: Role as the Mayor of Calcutta

Subhas Chandra Bose's ascension to the position of Mayor of Calcutta was a turning point in the city's history, heralding a new era of progressive governance and transformative policies. His tenure as Mayor was marked by a holistic approach to urban development, emphasising not just infrastructural improvements but also socio-economic upliftment and cultural enrichment.

1. **Urban Development and Infrastructure:**
   - **Roads and Bridges:** One of Bose's foremost priorities was the modernisation of Calcutta's road network. He spearheaded the construction of new arterial roads and the widening of existing ones to accommodate the increasing vehicular traffic. The development of strategic bridges, such as the construction of new spans over the Hooghly River, was undertaken to enhance connectivity and reduce congestion.
   - **Public Buildings:** Recognising the need for functional and aesthetic public spaces, Bose initiated the construction of several key public buildings. This included the establishment of modern municipal offices,

community centres, and public halls that served as venues for civic engagement and cultural events.
- **Drainage and Sewage Systems**: Calcutta's perennial flooding issues required urgent attention. Bose implemented comprehensive drainage and sewage projects, incorporating modern engineering solutions to manage rainwater runoff and waste disposal effectively. These initiatives significantly reduced the incidence of waterborne diseases and improved the overall public health scenario.

2. **Public Health and Sanitation**:
   - **Epidemic Control**: Bose's tenure saw proactive measures to combat epidemics such as cholera and malaria, which were rampant in the region. He launched extensive public health campaigns, including mass vaccination drives and awareness programs on hygiene practices. Health inspectors were deployed across the city to ensure compliance with sanitary regulations.
   - **Sanitary Reforms**: A significant focus was placed on improving the city's sanitary conditions. Bose introduced modern waste management practices, including the systematic collection and disposal of garbage. Public toilets and sanitation facilities were constructed in densely populated areas, ensuring access to basic amenities for all citizens.
   - **Healthcare Facilities**: Bose's vision for a healthy Calcutta included the establishment of healthcare facilities accessible to the general populace. New hospitals and clinics were built, equipped with the latest medical technologies. Special programs were launched to provide free or subsidised healthcare to the economically disadvantaged sections of society.

3. **Education and Libraries**:
   - **Expansion of Educational Institutions**: Bose's belief in education as a catalyst for social change led to the expansion of the city's educational infrastructure. Numerous schools were established, catering to children from all socio-economic backgrounds. Emphasis was placed on ensuring quality education, with well-trained teachers and modern curricula.
   - **Promotion of Female Education**: Bose was a staunch advocate for women's education, recognising its role in societal progress. Initiatives were launched to encourage female enrollment in schools and higher educational institutions. Scholarships and financial aid were provided to meritorious female students to support their academic pursuits.
   - **Public Libraries**: To foster a culture of learning and intellectual growth, Bose established public libraries across the city. These libraries became hubs of knowledge, offering a vast collection of books, journals, and periodicals. Special reading programs and literary events were organised to engage the community and promote a love for reading.
4. **Cultural and Social Initiatives**:
   - **Support for the Arts**: Bose's tenure as Mayor saw a cultural renaissance in Calcutta. He patronised local artists, musicians, and theatre groups, providing them with platforms to showcase their talents. Festivals, art exhibitions, and cultural events were organised to celebrate the city's rich artistic heritage.
   - **Promotion of Communal Harmony**: Calcutta, with its diverse population, often faced communal tensions. Bose's administration worked tirelessly to promote

communal harmony and understanding. Interfaith dialogues and community-building activities were organised to foster a sense of unity and mutual respect among different religious and ethnic groups.
- **Social Welfare Programs**: Bose introduced several social welfare programs aimed at improving the living conditions of the underprivileged. These included initiatives for the homeless, the establishment of orphanages, and support for the elderly. Programs were also launched to address issues such as child labour and to provide vocational training to marginalised communities.

5. **Economic Reforms**:
   - **Promotion of Small-Scale Industries**: Bose recognised the potential of small-scale industries in boosting the local economy and creating employment opportunities. He launched programs to support local artisans and craftsmen, providing them with financial assistance and market access. Efforts were made to promote traditional crafts and industries, ensuring their sustainability and growth.
   - **Labour Reforms**: Improving the working conditions of labourers was a key focus of Bose's economic reforms. He advocated for fair wages, safe working environments, and the establishment of labour rights. Trade unions were encouraged to participate in dialogues with employers to negotiate better terms and conditions for workers.
   - **Market Development**: Bose's administration worked on developing local markets and improving their infrastructure. This included the construction of modern marketplaces with adequate facilities for

vendors and buyers. Programs were launched to support local entrepreneurs and small businesses, fostering a vibrant and dynamic economic environment.

Contributions to Municipal Reforms

Bose's contributions to municipal reforms were multifaceted and aimed at creating a responsive, transparent, and efficient civic administration.

1. **Administrative Overhaul**:
   - **Streamlining Processes**: Bose undertook a comprehensive review of municipal processes to identify and eliminate inefficiencies. He introduced streamlined procedures for various civic services, reducing bureaucratic delays and enhancing service delivery. The adoption of modern administrative practices ensured greater accountability and transparency.
   - **Training and Capacity Building**: Recognising the need for a skilled workforce, Bose initiated training programs for municipal employees. Workshops and seminars were organised to enhance their skills and knowledge, equipping them to handle the complexities of urban governance effectively. Emphasis was placed on ethical practices and customer service.
   - **Performance Monitoring**: Bose introduced systems for regular performance monitoring and evaluation of municipal departments. Key performance indicators were established to measure the effectiveness of various programs and initiatives. This data-driven approach enabled timely interventions and course corrections, ensuring the optimal use of resources.

2. **Citizen Engagement**:
   - **Public Consultations**: Bose believed in participatory governance and actively sought the involvement of citizens in decision-making processes. Public consultations were organised to gather feedback on proposed policies and projects. Citizens were encouraged to voice their concerns and suggestions, fostering a sense of ownership and collaboration.
   - **Community Committees**: To enhance local governance, Bose established community committees at the neighbourhood level. These committees served as intermediaries between the municipal administration and the residents, addressing local issues and facilitating the implementation of civic programs. Regular meetings and dialogues were held to ensure effective communication and coordination.
   - **Civic Education**: Bose launched civic education campaigns to raise awareness about the rights and responsibilities of citizens. Educational programs, workshops, and information campaigns were organised to empower residents with the knowledge needed to actively participate in civic life. Special efforts were made to engage marginalised and underrepresented groups.
3. **Fiscal Reforms**:
   - **Efficient Resource Management**: Bose's fiscal reforms focused on the efficient management of municipal resources. Budgetary allocations were optimised to ensure the judicious use of funds. Measures were implemented to curb wastage and reduce unnecessary expenditures, enabling the redirection of resources to priority areas.
   - **Revenue Generation**: To increase municipal revenue,

Bose introduced innovative methods for tax collection and resource mobilisation. Property taxes, business licences, and service fees were rationalised to enhance compliance and ensure fairness. Efforts were made to broaden the tax base by identifying and including previously untapped revenue sources.
- **Financial Transparency**: Bose emphasised financial transparency and accountability. Regular audits and public disclosure of financial statements were mandated to build trust and confidence among citizens. The adoption of transparent financial practices ensured the integrity of municipal finances and minimised the risk of corruption.

4. **Innovative Programs**:
    - **Clean Calcutta Campaign**: One of Bose's flagship programs was the 'Clean Calcutta' campaign, aimed at transforming the city into a model of cleanliness and hygiene. The campaign mobilised citizens, schools, businesses, and community organisations to participate in cleanliness drives. Public awareness programs were conducted to promote responsible waste disposal and environmental stewardship.
    - **Green Initiatives**: Bose's administration prioritised environmental sustainability. Programs were launched to increase green cover through tree plantation drives and the creation of urban parks and gardens. Efforts were made to promote eco-friendly practices, such as waste segregation, recycling, and the use of renewable energy sources.
    - **Smart City Projects**: Bose's vision for a modern Calcutta included the adoption of smart city technologies. Initiatives were undertaken to integrate digital solutions

into urban management, such as the implementation of smart traffic systems, e-governance platforms, and public Wi-Fi networks. These projects aimed to enhance the efficiency and convenience of civic services.

Conflict and Alliance with Other Leaders

Relationship with C.R. Das and Jawaharlal Nehru

Subhas Chandra Bose's political journey was profoundly influenced by his interactions with other key figures of the Indian independence movement. His relationships with Chittaranjan Das (C.R. Das) and Jawaharlal Nehru were particularly significant, shaping his ideological development and strategic approaches.

1. **Mentorship of C.R. Das**:
   - **Early Interaction and Influence**: Bose's association with C.R. Das began in the early 1920s when Das was already a prominent leader in Bengal and a staunch advocate for Swaraj (self-rule). Das recognized Bose's potential and took him under his wing, providing him with invaluable guidance and mentorship. This relationship profoundly influenced Bose's political beliefs and strategies.
   - **Political Ideologies**: Das's emphasis on inclusive and pragmatic politics resonated with Bose. Das advocated for a balanced approach that combined non-violent resistance with active participation in legislative processes. Bose adopted this dual strategy, emphasizing both grassroots mobilization and institutional engagement.
   - **Organisational Skills**: Under Das's mentorship, Bose honed his organisational skills. He was entrusted with

significant responsibilities within the Swarajya Party, which Das co-founded. Bose's ability to mobilise support, coordinate activities, and execute plans effectively can be attributed to the rigourous training and mentorship he received from Das.

2. **Ideological Synergy and Differences with Jawaharlal Nehru**:
   - **Shared Vision of Modern India**: Bose and Nehru shared a common vision of a free, secular, and progressive India. Both leaders were influenced by socialist ideals and believed in the need for economic and social reforms to achieve true independence. Their collaborative efforts were evident in their joint initiatives to promote industrialization, education, and social justice.
   - **Mutual Respect and Collaboration**: Despite their differences, Bose and Nehru maintained a relationship of mutual respect and collaboration. They often engaged in constructive debates, challenging each other's views while working towards common objectives. Their ability to reconcile their differences and cooperate on key issues was a testament to their dedication to the cause of India's freedom.

Formation of the Swarajya Party

The formation of the Swarajya Party marked a pivotal chapter in Bose's political career, showcasing his strategic acumen and leadership skills.

1. **Context and Rationale**:
   - **Dissatisfaction with British Policies**: The early 1920s saw growing dissatisfaction with British colonial

policies, particularly after the repressive measures taken in response to the Non-Cooperation Movement. Leaders like C.R. Das and Motilal Nehru felt the need for a more structured and constitutional approach to challenge British authority.

- **Need for Legislative Representation**: The Swarajya Party was conceived as a platform to enter legislative councils and work within the British constitutional framework to push for self-governance. The party aimed to use legislative representation as a means to voice the aspirations of the Indian populace and hold the British administration accountable.

2. **Bose's Role in the Party**:
   - **Mobilising Support**: Bose played a crucial role in mobilising support for the Swarajya Party. His charismatic leadership and eloquent speeches attracted a broad base of followers, particularly among the youth and intellectuals. Bose's ability to inspire and galvanize the masses was instrumental in building a strong organisational network for the party.
   - **Organisational Leadership**: As a key member of the Swarajya Party, Bose was actively involved in organizing party activities and strategies. He coordinated with regional leaders to establish a cohesive strategy for contesting elections and promoting the party's agenda. Bose's administrative acumen ensured efficient execution of plans and programs.
   - **Advocacy and Propaganda**: Bose's role extended to advocacy and propaganda, where he utilized various platforms to propagate the party's message. He wrote extensively in newspapers and journals, articulating the party's vision and policies. His writings and speeches

played a significant role in shaping public opinion and garnering support for the party.

3. **Electoral Strategy and Successes:**
   - **Election Campaigns:** The Swarajya Party's electoral strategy involved meticulous planning and grassroots mobilization. Bose led several election campaigns, traveling extensively to garner support. The party's manifesto emphasised self-governance, civil liberties, and socio-economic reforms, resonating with a wide section of the populace.
   - **Electoral Victories:** The party's success in the 1923 elections was a testament to its effective strategy and popular support. The Swarajya Party won a significant number of seats in the Central Legislative Assembly and provincial legislatures. Bose's leadership was critical in these victories, showcasing his ability to navigate the political landscape effectively.
   - **Legislative Activism:** Once in power, the Swarajya Party members engaged in legislative activism, using their positions to challenge British policies and advocate for Indian interests. Bose played a key role in drafting and supporting legislative proposals aimed at enhancing civil liberties, promoting social justice, and pushing for economic reforms.
4. **Impact on the Independence Movement:**
   - **Strategic Shift:** The formation and success of the Swarajya Party marked a strategic shift in the Indian independence movement. It demonstrated the potential of constitutional methods in challenging British authority and achieving self-governance. The party's approach provided a viable alternative to the non-cooperation and civil disobedience strategies,

broadening the movement's appeal.
- **Legacy of Legislative Engagement**: The Swarajya Party's legacy of legislative engagement had a lasting impact on the Indian political landscape. It paved the way for future political strategies that combined grassroots mobilization with institutional participation. The party's efforts also highlighted the importance of democratic processes and the rule of law in achieving political objectives.
- **Bose's Political Evolution**: Bose's involvement in the Swarajya Party significantly shaped his political evolution. The experience of working within the legislative framework, engaging with diverse political ideologies, and navigating the complexities of coalition politics enriched his understanding of governance and strategy. This period was instrumental in shaping his future leadership roles and political philosophy.

Netaji Subhas Chandra Bose's 125th Birth Anniversary stamp

Credits: India Post, Government of India, GODL-India <https:// data.gov.in/sites/default/files/ Gazette_Notification_OGDL.pdf>, via Wikimedia Commons

Subhas Chandra Bose's rise to prominence was characterised by his innovative leadership in Bengal, his complex relationships with other key leaders, and his pivotal role in the formation and success of the Swarajya Party. His contributions during this period were instrumental in shaping the trajectory of the Indian independence movement and left a lasting legacy on the nation's political landscape. Bose's visionary leadership, strategic acumen, and unwavering commitment to the cause of India's freedom continue to inspire generations.

5

1921–1932: INDIAN NATIONAL CONGRESS

Subhas Chandra Bose's political career in the Indian National Congress (INC) began to take shape as he aligned himself with the vision of aggressive nationalism advocated by his mentor, Chittaranjan Das. Bose launched the newspaper Swaraj and took charge of publicity for the Bengal Provincial Congress Committee. Das, a prominent figure in Bengal's political landscape, became Bose's guiding force, shaping his approach to the struggle for independence.

In 1923, Bose's influence within the Congress grew as he was elected the President of the All India Youth Congress and the Secretary of the Bengal State Congress. His role as editor of the newspaper Forward, founded by Das, further established his prominence in the nationalist movement. When Das was elected mayor of Calcutta in 1924, Bose served as the CEO of the Calcutta Municipal Corporation, demonstrating his administrative capabilities

A drawing by the artist Beohar Rammanohar Sinha, supplemented and detailed by his mentor master–moshai Nandalal Bose, on page 160 of the original Constitution of India.

A drawing by the artist Beohar Rammanohar Sinha, detailed by his colleagues Avtar Singh, Sovon Som, Sukhen Ganguly, as a mural in Shaheed-Smarak Concert-hall, Jabalpur MP, India.

Subhas Chandra Bose_INA

Credits: Beohar Rammanohar Sinha, Public domain, via Wikimedia Commons

and commitment to civic leadership.

However, the British colonial authorities viewed Bose's rising influence and nationalistic activities with suspicion. In 1925, during a crackdown on nationalist leaders, Bose was arrested and imprisoned in Mandalay, Burma (now Myanmar). The harsh conditions of his imprisonment led to a bout with tuberculosis, but this did not dampen his resolve.

> **Fun Fact:**
> **Bose and Congress Socialist Party:** Bose had close ties with the Congress Socialist Party, aligning with leaders like Jayaprakash Narayan and Ram Manohar Lohia, who shared his radical views.

After his release in 1927, Bose resumed his active role in the Congress, becoming the party's general secretary. He collaborated closely with Jawaharlal Nehru, another prominent leader in the struggle for independence. Together, they worked tirelessly to galvanize the masses and build momentum for the freedom movement.

> **Fun Fact:**
> **Prison Sentences:** Bose was imprisoned multiple times by the British for his revolutionary activities. His time in prison only strengthened his resolve to fight for India's independence.

Bose's organisational skills were on full display during the Annual Meeting of the Indian National Congress in Calcutta in December 1928. As General Officer Commanding (GOC) of the Congress Volunteer Corps, he orchestrated a disciplined and impressive assembly of volunteers. The sight of volunteers in uniform, complete with steel-cut epaulettes, created a stir. British General in Fort William even received a telegram addressed to Bose as GOC, which caused considerable gossip in the British Indian press. This militaristic display, however, did not sit well with Mahatma Gandhi, who was committed to non-violence and viewed the spectacle as reminiscent of a circus, causing some friction between Bose and the more pacifist factions within the Congress.

Despite the differences in approach, Bose's dedication to the cause remained unwavering. In 1930, he was once again arrested for participating in civil disobedience activities. Upon his release, he continued to serve his city and country, becoming the Mayor of Calcutta, a position that allowed him to influence local governance and implement his vision of a self-reliant India.

Mid-1930s: European Sojourn and Political Observations

The mid-1930s marked a period of extensive travel and intellectual growth for Bose. He journeyed across Europe, meeting with Indian students and engaging with influential European politicians,

Subhas Chandra Bose Statue at Vadodara, Gujarat

Credits: Snehrashmi, CC BY-SA 4.0 <https://creativecommons.org/licenses/by-sa/4.0>, via Wikimedia Commons

including Benito Mussolini. These interactions provided Bose with a broader perspective on global political ideologies and party organisations. He observed the functioning of communism and fascism firsthand, analysing their methods and strategies.

During this period, Bose also focused on his literary pursuits, researching and writing the first part of his book, *The Indian Struggle*. This seminal work documented the Indian independence movement from 1920 to 1934, providing a detailed account of the efforts, challenges, and aspirations of the nationalist leaders and the masses. Although published in London in 1935, the British government banned the book in India, fearing that its contents might incite further unrest and strengthen the resolve of the freedom fighters.

Bose's time in Europe was not just about political observations and literary work; it also involved forging connections and seeking support for India's cause on an international stage. His efforts to garner international backing and his strategic observations of different political systems underscored his pragmatic approach to achieving India's independence.

Subhas Chandra Bose's journey from the early 1920s to the mid-1930s was marked by relentless dedication to the Indian independence movement, profound intellectual growth, and significant political activity. His integration of Western education and Indian spiritual philosophy provided him with a distinct viewpoint, merging analytical reasoning with a deep sense of responsibility towards his nation. This powerful synthesis not only defined his personal journey but also significantly influenced the broader struggle for India's independence. Bose's ability to navigate the complexities of both Indian and global political landscapes made him a formidable leader, whose legacy continues to inspire generations. His life exemplifies the transformative power of education, spirituality, and unwavering commitment to one's duty to humanity and the nation.

6

1937–1940: INDIAN NATIONAL CONGRESS

In 1938, Subhas Chandra Bose articulated his vision that the Indian National Congress (INC) "should be organised on the broadest anti-imperialist front with the two-fold objective of winning political freedom and the establishment of a socialist regime." By then, Bose had risen to national prominence and accepted the nomination for Congress President. He championed unqualified Swaraj (self-governance), advocating the use of force against the British if necessary. This position put him in direct confrontation with Mohandas Gandhi, who opposed Bose's presidency, thereby creating a schism within the INC.

> **Fun Fact:**
> **Statue in India Gate:** A grand statue of Subhas Chandra Bose is planned to be installed at India Gate, New Delhi, symbolising his pivotal role in India's independence movement.

Despite Bose's efforts to maintain unity within the party, Gandhi advised him to form his own cabinet, which further deepened the rift. This division also strained Bose's relationship with Jawaharlal Nehru. At the 1939 Congress meeting, Bose, appearing on a stretcher due to his failing health, was re-elected as president over Gandhi's preferred candidate, Pattabhi Sitaramayya. U. Muthuramalingam Thevar played a crucial role in securing Bose's victory by mobilising support from South India. However, the maneuverings of the Gandhi-led faction within the Congress Working Committee ultimately forced Bose to resign from the presidency.

On June 22, 1939, Bose established the All India Forward Bloc, a faction within the INC aimed at consolidating the political left, though its primary strength lay in Bengal. U. Muthuramalingam Thevar, a staunch supporter, joined the Forward Bloc and organized a massive rally in Madurai to welcome Bose on September 6, 1939.

During his travels to Madurai, Bose stopped in Madras, spending three days at Gandhi Peak. His correspondence from this period reveals his admiration for the British methodical and systematic approach to governance and their disciplined outlook on life, despite his clear opposition to British rule. In England, Bose exchanged ideas with British Labour Party leaders and political thinkers such as Lord Halifax, George Lansbury, Clement Attlee, Arthur Greenwood, Harold Laski, J.B.S. Haldane, Ivor Jennings, G.D.H. Cole, Gilbert Murray, and Sir Stafford Cripps.

Subhas Chandra Bose, Indian nationalist and prominent figure of the Indian independence movement.

Bose came to believe that an independent India would require socialist authoritarianism, akin to the model established by Turkey's Kemal Atatürk, for at least two decades. For political reasons, the British authorities denied Bose permission to meet Atatürk in Ankara. During his sojourn in England, Bose attempted to engage with several politicians, but only the Labour and Liberal Party members agreed to meet him. Conservative Party officials refused to show him courtesy, viewing him merely as a colonial politician. This refusal was indicative of the broader Conservative opposition to even Dominion status for India during the 1930s. It was under the Labour Party government, led by Prime Minister Attlee from 1945 to 1951, that India ultimately gained independence.

With the outbreak of World War II, Bose advocated for a campaign of mass civil disobedience to protest against Viceroy Lord Linlithgow's unilateral decision to declare war on India's behalf without consulting Congress leadership. Failing to convince Gandhi of the necessity of this action, Bose organized mass protests in Calcutta, calling for the removal of the 'Holwell Monument,' which commemorated the Black Hole of Calcutta and stood at the corner of Dalhousie Square. His defiance led to his imprisonment by the British authorities. However, following a seven-day hunger strike, Bose was released, but his house in Calcutta remained under constant surveillance by the Criminal Investigation Department (CID).

Subhas Chandra Bose, Former Head of State and Prime Minister of the Provisional Government of Free India

Bose's relentless drive and uncompromising stance against British imperialism during this period cemented his status as a key figure in India's struggle for independence. His efforts to forge a path of direct action and his advocacy for a socialist regime resonated with many Indians, inspiring a new wave of fervour for the nationalist cause. His experiences in Europe, interactions with global political thinkers, and unwavering commitment to India's freedom laid the groundwork for his later endeavours, including his leadership of the Indian National Army and his continued fight against colonial rule.

Subhas Chandra Bose's journey from 1937 to 1940 was marked by significant political activity, ideological evolution, and relentless advocacy for India's independence. His vision of an organized, anti-imperialist front, his leadership within the INC, and his establishment of the All India Forward Bloc exemplify his strategic and determined approach to achieving self-governance. Bose's ability to blend intellectual rigour, political strategy, and a profound sense of duty towards his country established him as a pivotal figure in the history of India's independence movement. His legacy, characterised by sacrifice, resilience, and an unyielding commitment to freedom, continues to inspire future generations.

> **Fun Fact:**
>
> **Influence on Youth:** Bose's charismatic personality and fiery speeches inspired a generation of young Indians to join the freedom struggle, making him a beloved leader among the youth.

7

1941–1943: NAZI GERMANY

Bose's arrest and subsequent release set the scene for his escape to Germany, via Afghanistan and the Soviet Union. A few days before his escape, he sought solitude and, on this pretext, avoided meeting British guards and grew a beard. Late night 16 January 1941, the night of his escape, he dressed as a Pathan (brown long coat, a black fez-type coat and broad pyjamas) to avoid being identified. Bose escaped from under British surveillance from his Elgin Road house in Calcutta on the night of 17 January 1941, accompanied by his nephew Sisir Kumar Bose, later reaching Gomoh Railway Station in then state of Bihar, India.

He journeyed to Peshawar with the help of the Abwehr, where he was met by Akbar Shah, Mohammed Shah and Bhagat Ram Talwar. Bose was taken to the home of Abad Khan, a trusted friend of Akbar Shah's. On 26 January 1941, Bose began his journey to reach Russia through British India's North West frontier with Afghanistan.

Photo of Subhas Chandra Bose in Cambridge in 1919 displayed at Netaji Museum and Centre for Studies in Himalayan Languages Society & Culture, Giddha Pahar, Darjeeling district, West Bengal.

For this reason, he enlisted the help of Mian Akbar Shah, then a Forward Bloc leader in the North-West Frontier Province. Shah had been out of India en route to the Soviet Union, and suggested a novel disguise for Bose to assume. Since Bose could not speak one word of Pashto, it would make him an easy target of Pashto speakers working for the British. For this reason, Shah suggested that Bose act deaf and dumb, and let his beard grow to mimic those of the tribesmen. Bose's guide Bhagat Ram Talwar, unknown to him, was a Soviet agent.

> **Fun Fact:**
> **Indian National Congress President (Tripuri):** Bose was re-elected as the Congress President in 1939 at the Tripuri Session but resigned due to differences with Gandhi and the Congress Working Committee.

Supporters of the Aga Khan III helped him across the border into Afghanistan where he was met by an Abwehr unit posing as a party of road construction engineers from the Organisation Todt who then aided his passage across Afghanistan via Kabul to the border with Soviet Russia. After assuming the guise of a Pashtun insurance agent ("Ziaudddin") to reach Afghanistan, Bose changed his guise and travelled to Moscow on the Italian passport of an Italian nobleman "Count Orlando Mazzotta". From Moscow, he reached Rome, and from there he travelled to Germany. Once in Russia the NKVD transported Bose to Moscow where he hoped that Russia's traditional enmity to British rule in India would result in support for his plans for a popular rising in India. However, Bose found the

Netaji Subhas Chandra Bose Gomoh Railway Station

Credits: Raxit Gupta, CC BY-SA 3.0 <https://creativecommons.org/licenses/by-sa/3.0>, via Wikimedia Commons

Soviets' response disappointing and was rapidly passed over to the German Ambassador in Moscow, Count von der Schulenburg. He had Bose flown on to Berlin in a special courier aircraft at the beginning of April where he was to receive a more favourable hearing from Joachim von Ribbentrop and the Foreign Ministry officials at the Wilhelmstrasse.

In Germany, he was attached to the Special Bureau for India under Adam von Trott zu Solz which was responsible for broadcasting on the German-sponsored Azad Hind Radio. He founded the Free India Center in Berlin, and created the Indian Legion (consisting of some 4500 soldiers) out of Indian prisoners of war who had previously fought for the British in North Africa prior to their capture by Axis forces. The Indian Legion was attached to the Wehrmacht, and later transferred to the Waffen SS. Its members swore the following allegiance to Hitler and Bose: "I swear by God this holy oath that I will obey the leader of the German race and state, Adolf Hitler, as the commander of the German armed forces in the fight for India, whose leader is Subhas Chandra Bose". This oath clearly abrogates control of the Indian legion to the German armed forces whilst stating Bose's overall leadership of India. He was also, however, prepared to envisage an invasion of India via the USSR by Nazi troops, spearheaded by the Azad Hind Legion; many have questioned his judgment here, as it seems unlikely that the Germans could have been

Portrait of Indian revolutionary Subhas Chandra Bose on a postcard.

Credits: Rajni, CC BY 4.0 <https://creativecommons.org/licenses/by/4.0>, via Wikimedia Commons

easily persuaded to leave after such an invasion, which might also have resulted in an Axis victory in the War.

In all, 3,000 Indian prisoners of war signed up for the Free India Legion. But instead of being delighted, Bose was worried. A left-wing admirer of Russia, he was devastated when Hitler's tanks rolled across the Soviet border. Matters were worsened by the fact that the now-retreating German army would be in no position to offer him help in driving the British from India. When he met Hitler in May 1942, his suspicions were confirmed, and he came to believe that the Nazi leader was more interested in using his men to win propaganda victories than military ones. So, in February 1943, Bose boarded a German U-Boat and left for Japan. This left the men he had recruited leaderless and demoralized in Germany.

> **Fun Fact:**
>
> **Escape in Disguise:** Bose's escape from India involved disguising himself as a Pathan to avoid British surveillance. This adventurous journey exemplifies his daring spirit.

Bose lived in Berlin from 1941 until 1943. During his earlier visit to Germany in 1934, he had met Emilie Schenkl, the daughter of an Austrian veterinarian whom he married in 1937. Their daughter is Anita Bose Pfaff. Bose's party, the Forward Bloc, has contested this fact.

8

1943–1945: JAPANESE-OCCUPIED ASIA

In 1943, after becoming disillusioned that Germany could help gain India's independence, he left for Japan. He travelled with the German submarine U-180 around the Cape of Good Hope to the southeast of Madagascar, where he was transferred to the I-29 for the rest of the journey to Imperial Japan. This was the only civilian transfer between two submarines of two different navies in World War II.

The Indian National Army (INA) was the brainchild of Japanese Major (and post-war Lieutenant-General) Iwaichi

Subhas Chandra Bose in Germany Date between 1930 and 1945

Fujiwara, head the Japanese intelligence unit Fujiwara Kikan and had its origins, first in the meetings between Fujiwara and the president of the Bangkok chapter of the Indian Independence League, Pritam Singh Dhillon, and then, through Pritam Singh's network, in the recruitment by Fujiwara of a captured British Indian army captain, Mohan Singh on the western Malayan peninsula in December 1941; Fujiwara's mission was "to raise an army which would fight alongside the Japanese army." After the initial proposal by Fujiwara the Indian National Army was formed as a result of discussion between Fujiwara and Mohan Singh in the second half of December 1941, and the name chosen jointly by them in the first week of January 1942.

> **Fun Fact:**
> **Alliance with Japan:** Bose's alliance with Japan during World War II was a strategic move to garner support for India's independence, highlighting his pragmatic approach to international politics.

This was along the concept of—and with support of—what was then known as the Indian Independence League, headed by expatriate nationalist leader Rash Behari Bose. The first INA was however disbanded in December 1942 after disagreements between the Hikari Kikan and Mohan Singh, who came to believe that the Japanese High Command was using the INA as a mere pawn and propaganda tool. Mohan Singh was taken into custody and the troops returned to the prisoner-of-war camp. However, the idea of an independence army was revived with the arrival of Subhas Chandra Bose in the Far East in 1943. In July, at a meeting in Singapore, Rash Behari Bose handed over control of the organisation to Subhas Chandra Bose. Bose was able to reorganise the fledgling army and organise massive support among the expatriate Indian population in south-east

Asia, who lent their support by both enlisting in the Indian National Army, as well as financially in response to Bose's calls for sacrifice for the independence cause. INA had a separate women's unit, the Rani of Jhansi Regiment (named after Rani Lakshmi Bai) headed by Capt. Lakshmi Swaminathan, which is seen as a first of its kind in Asia.

Even when faced with military reverses, Bose was able to maintain support for the Azad Hind movement. Spoken as a part of a motivational speech for the Indian National Army at a rally of Indians in Burma on 4 July 1944, Bose's most famous quote was "Give me blood, and I shall give you freedom!" In this, he urged the people of India to join him in his fight against the British Raj. Spoken in Hindi, Bose's words are highly evocative. The troops of the INA were under the aegis of a provisional government, the Azad Hind Government, which came to produce its own currency, postage stamps, court and civil code, and was recognised by nine Axis states–Germany,

Subhas Chandra Bose in Germany.

Japan, Italian Social Republic, the Independent State of Croatia, Wang Jingwei regime in Nanjing, China, a provisional government of Burma, Manchukuo and Japanese-controlled Philippines. Recent researches have shown that the USSR too had diplomatic contact with the "Provisional Government of Free India". Of those countries, five were authorities established under Axis occupation. This government participated in the so-called Greater East Asia Conference as an observer in November 1943.

The INA's first commitment was in the Japanese thrust towards Eastern Indian frontiers of Manipur. INA's special forces, the Bahadur Group, were extensively involved in operations behind enemy lines both during the diversionary attacks in Arakan, as well as the Japanese thrust towards Imphal and Kohima, along with the Burmese National Army led by Ba Maw and Aung San.

The Japanese also took possession of Andaman and Nicobar Islands in 1942 and a year later, the Provisional Government and the INA were established in the Andaman and Nicobar Islands with Lt Col. A.D. Loganathan appointed its Governor General. The islands were renamed Shaheed (Martyr) and Swaraj (Independence). However, the Japanese Navy remained in essential control of the island's administration. During Bose's only visit to the islands in early 1944, apparently in the interest of shielding Bose from attaining a full knowledge of ultimate Japanese intentions, Bose's Japanese hosts carefully isolated him from the local population. At that time the island's Japanese administration had been torturing the leader of the island's Indian Independence League, Dr. Diwan Singh, who later died of his injuries in the Cellular Jail. During Bose's visit to the islands several locals attempted to alert Bose to Dr. Singh's plight, but apparently without success. During this time Lt. Col Loganathan became aware of his lack of any genuine administrative control and resigned in protest as Governor General, later returning to the Government's headquarters in Rangoon.

On the Indian mainland, an Indian Tricolour, modelled after that of the Indian National Congress, was raised for the first time in the town of Moirang, in Manipur, in north-eastern India. The adjacent towns of Kohima and Imphal were then encircled and placed under siege by divisions of the Japanese Army, working in conjunction with the Burmese National Army, and with Brigades of the INA, known as the Gandhi and Nehru Brigades. This attempt at conquering the Indian mainland had the Axis codename of Operation U-Go.

During this operation, On 6 July 1944, in a speech broadcast by the Azad Hind Radio from Singapore, Bose addressed Mahatma Gandhi as the "Father of the Nation" and asked for his blessings and good wishes for the war he was fighting. This was the first time that Gandhi was referred to by this appellation. [82] The protracted Japanese attempts to take these two towns depleted Japanese resources, with Operation U-Go ultimately proving unsuccessful. Through several months of Japanese onslaught on these two towns, Commonwealth forces remained entrenched in the towns. Commonwealth forces then counter-attacked, inflicting serious losses on the Axis led forces, who were then forced into a retreat back into Burmese territory. After the Japanese defeat at the battles of Kohima and Imphal, Bose's Provisional Government's aim of establishing a base in mainland India was lost forever.

Subhas Chandra Bose 1993 stamp of India

Credits: India Post, Government of India, GODL-India <https://data.gov.in/sites/default/files/Gazette_Notification_OGDL.pdf>, via Wikimedia Commons

Still the INA fought in key battles against the British Indian Army in Burmese territory, notable in Meiktilla, Mandalay, Pegu, Nyangyu and Mount Popa. However, with the fall of Rangoon, Bose's government ceased to be an effective political entity. A large proportion of the INA troops surrendered under Lt Col Loganathan. The remaining troops retreated with Bose towards Malaya or made for Thailand. Japan's surrender at the end of the war also led to the surrender of the remaining elements of the Indian National Army. The INA prisoners were then repatriated to India and some tried for treason.